PATHWAY
To the Heart
of GOD

"God's Blueprint
For Spiritual Maturity"

Light of the World Publishers
Nashville, TN

PATHWAY To the Heart of GOD

Published by
   Light of the World Publishers
   4020 Jordonia Station Road
   Nashville, TN 37218
   e-mail: Don@afellowtravelor.com
   Website: www.afellowtravelor.com

International Standard Book Number:
0-9675485-1-9
First Printing 2004

Art Direction by
   McClearen Design Studios
   Nashville, TN

* Scriptures are taken from the King James Version of the bible.
* Greek and Hebrew translations are from Strong's Exhaustive
   Concordance.

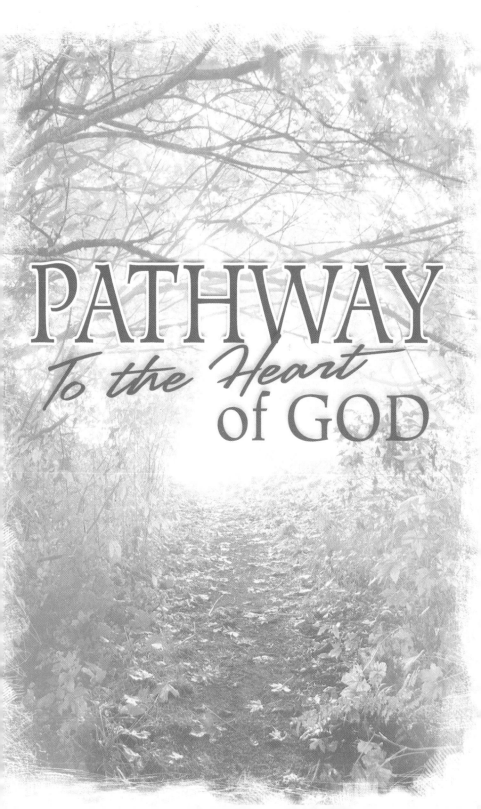

Table of Contents

Jesus Christ Loves You and Will Never Give Up On You

No matter what you do to yourself, to your loved ones, to your enemies, Jesus Christ loves you and will never give up on you.

His love is always reaching out to you. All you must do to receive this Love is to accept His Love. Say this now, say it out loud if possible. "Thank you Jesus. I accept your Love. I accept your will for my life."

Jesus Christ died for your sins and thereby gave you eternal life. Now tell our Lord you accept His free gift of eternal life and surrender your will to His will.

All through the day repeat over and over "Thank you Jesus," and Jesus will give you inner peace that will surpass your most cherished earthly dreams.

Jesus Christ is alive today and the Bible is "The Word". Admit your needs, accept Him into your life and change your world. Read the word of God daily and learn the truth.

Jim Hunt,
Chairman
Buffet Pizza Company, LLC
jhunt@buffetpizza.com

How to Walk God's **PATH**
To His Abundant Life and Blessings

From the Author,

It is apparent from scripture that there is a **PATH** that we are to walk if we are to receive God's abundant blessings.

....."The **PATH** of the just is as the shining light that shineth more and more unto the perfect day!" (Proverbs 4:18)

....."Thy word is a lamp unto my feet and a light unto my **PATH**." (Psalm 119:105)

....."Thou will show me the **PATH** of life. In Thy presence is fullness of joy. At Thy right hand there are pleasures forever more." (Psalm 16:11)

The purpose of walking God's **PATH** of situations, circumstances, trials, failures, pruning and blessings is that God may get us to a place where self is dead. Only then can the Triune Godhead, as seen in the life of Jesus, be manifested in and through us to a lost and dying world by the power of the Holy Spirit.

....."We all, with open face, beholding as in a glass (mirror) the glory of the Lord, are changed into the same image from glory to glory, even as by the spirit of the Lord."

(2 Corinthians 3:18)

By the enlightenment of the Holy Spirit, this book will show you the simple steps that God requires in order for us to walk **HIS PATH**. Our prayer should be "Show me Thy ways O Lord, teach me Thy **PATH**".

(Psalm 25:4)

WARNING!

THE **PATH** WILL BE SO MUCH EASIER
IF WE WILL MAKE THIS DECISION
BEFORE WE START OUT ON IT!

"I WILL TRUST IN THE LORD WITH **ALL** OF MY HEART AND LEAN NOT UNTO MY OWN UNDERSTANDING. IN **ALL** OF MY WAYS, I WILL ACKNOWLEDGE HIM (AND HIS AUTHORITY), AND HE SHALL DIRECT MY **PATH**."   (PROVERBS 3:5-6)

THE **PATH** WILL BE MUCH MORE EXCITING AND FULL OF GOD'S MIRACULOUS POWER IF WE TRUST GOD'S LOVE FOR ALL OF OUR NEEDS. (PHILIPPIANS 4:19)

GOD SPEAKING: "TRUST MY LOVE" MEANS... LET GO OF WHAT YOU WANT AND TRUST MY LOVE TO MAKE WHAT I WANT HAPPEN IN YOUR LIFE. YOU THEN ARE IN MY WILL AND ALL OF MY BLESSINGS WILL BE YOURS **NOW** AND FOR ALL ETERNITY."[33]

NOTE: The small number at the end of a sentence shows you the scripture in the back of the book (beginning on page 83) that the sentence relates to.

Please turn to the number listed and read the scripture. It will build your faith in God's love, a necessary weapon on the **PATH**. The letters H. and G. stand for the Hebrew and Greek section of Strong's Concordance.

GOD'S ASSURANCE

We Have This Assurance From Our Lord God As We Begin Our Journey.

"I WILL INSTRUCT THEE AND TEACH THEE IN THE WAY WHICH THOU SHALT GO. I WILL GUIDE THEE WITH MY EYE."
(PSALM 32:8)

If along the way, the path becomes difficult, confusing, dangerous or lonely; we can be encouraged with these words.

"The Lord is my shepherd, I shall not want!

"He maketh me to lie down in green pastures. He leadeth me beside the still waters.

"He restoreth my soul. He leadeth me in the **PATHS** of righteousness for His name's sake.

"Yea, though I walk through the valley of the shadow of death, I will fear no evil. For Thou art with me. Thy rod and Thy staff, they comfort me.

"Thou preparest a table before me in the presence of mine enemies. Thou anointest my head with oil. My cup runneth over.

"Surely goodness and mercy shall follow me all the days of my life and I will dwell in the house of the Lord forever."   (Psalm 23: 1-6)

Final Instructions for the Journey

As we start out on the path to God's blessings and abundance, it is important that we carry two pieces of information with us. Without this knowledge, the path will become too difficult, and as many have done before, we will turn back.

1. We must be willing to believe against all odds that God loves us and his **greatest desire** is to give us abundant blessings.[1]

2. We must understand how God works in our life, in order to get us to a point where He can give us all of His blessings right on this earth.

NOW, LET'S BEGIN OUR JOURNEY. TOGETHER WE WILL EXPERIENCE HOW TO WALK GOD'S **PATH**. WE WILL START WHERE I STARTED WHEN I FIRST MET JESUS AS SAVIOR.

Don Hunt,
A Fellow Traveler

Suggested Reading: Bruce Wilkinson's book, *The Prayer of Jabez,* will give you a strong foundation for #1 above. His book, *Secrets of the Vine,* will give you exactly what you need for #2. *Multnomah Publishers, Inc.*

He Turned My Mourning Into Dancing!

CHAPTER 1

The revelation that our Lord shared with me on how to walk His path to His abundant life and blessings began on June 4, 1974.

On that day, I decided to kill myself! Instead, as I sat alone in my den brooding in total despair, I became very mad at God! I had asked Him over and over to help me overcome the sins of the flesh. Yet, the world and the devil, combined with my own selfish desires continued to drag me into the pits of hell.

No matter how much I prayed, God had not helped me overcome these sins. I truly desired to overcome them. Since I was still held captive, I reasoned that God was not interested in helping me. Instead of killing myself, in tremendous anger, here is what I said to God. I said it out loud and I meant it!

"God, I don't love you! I don't like you and I don't even want to like you. But, I tell you what I am going to do. I <u>will</u> to give you my life. That doesn't mean I want to. I just <u>will</u> to do it! If you want my life, fine. If you don't, forget it. From now on, I am going to sit in this chair and do nothing else." (In other words, I am going to stop trying to be good enough to earn heaven.)

A Revelation

Praise God! God is a God of love. He loves each one of us so much. Even though I did not know it at the time, despite my unusual method of giving Him my life, He took it!

I had never studied the Bible. I did not know that Jesus said in Revelations 3:20 that He stands at the door (of our heart) and knocks. If <u>any</u> person will hear His voice, and open the door (of their heart), that He would come in.[2]

I thought I had to be good enough to earn my way to heaven. Since I could not control my fleshly lusts; I knew I was going to hell. No one (to my remembrance) had ever told me that we are saved by faith and not by works.[3]

Two days later on a business trip to Memphis, Tennessee, my new Lord and Savior Jesus Christ, began to reveal Himself to me.[4]

God's Message to Me

As I traveled the Memphis road, the Lord began to speak to me. It was a small quiet voice within me. Here is what I heard the Lord say.

"I love you! Your name is written in the Book of Life and you are going to spend eternity with Me in heaven. Not because you are good, but because I died on the cross for you and My blood washed you white as snow."

For a person who had talked about God all his life, but knew nothing about the salvation message, I got excited! When I heard our Lord's words, combined with the perfect peace that swept over me, I knew that I knew that I knew... that I was free from the punishment of sin forever.[5]

Then the Lord said, "This is the very last times. The devil is pouring out his filth like he has never done before, but I am pouring out my Spirit and not a single person need be lost except those who harden their heart."[6]

Then He said to me, "Do not talk about anything but **Love** and **Faith**." I now realize that if each member of the Body of Christ talked only of God's love for us and the importance of having faith in that love for all of our needs, we would quickly come into a unity of faith. Seeing Jesus in us, a great harvest of souls would soon follow.

Every Christian knows about love and faith. Yet, too few realize that each of these words is like a deep well in their true meaning. Many of us only drink from the top foot of water in each well, never realizing the pure living water of truth that is far below.

The Lord Jesus has made it very clear to me, through His word, that the true meaning of **Love** and **Faith** and its application in our every day life is the very core of His last day's message.

From the time the Lord spoke to me on the way to Memphis in June of 1974, until Easter morning of 1975, I had no idea what the Lord meant when He said I should talk only about love and faith. Then, on Easter morning, right before church services were to begin, the Lord quietly spoke the following words to me. "What I mean is ... you can have total faith in My love for all of your needs."

Praise God for His tremendous mercy! Please join me right now in giving praise and glory for His wonderful gifts to men. If you are unable to thank Him and praise Him for what He has done in your life, then you are really going to enjoy this book. It will show you the key to open the door of the blessings God wants to give you.

What a message to get to talk about. Quickly however, I found out that although the Lord had shown me what He meant by love and faith, I had much to learn about how to have total faith in God's love for all of my needs. Without realizing it, I had now received from our Lord the very truth that would not only make the Bride without spot or wrinkle, but would be the power that would fulfill Ephesians 4:13 and prepare the Body of Christ for a great harvest of souls and then our Lord's return.

"TILL WE ALL COME IN THE UNITY OF THE FAITH, AND OF THE KNOWLEDGE OF THE SON OF GOD, UNTO A PERFECT MAN, UNTO THE MEASURE OF THE STATURE OF THE FULLNESS OF CHRIST."

(EPHESIANS 4:13)

Getting Started On The Path

CHAPTER 2

The period between June, 1974 and Easter of 1975 was a real spiritual growth period for me. Immediately after the Memphis trip, our Lord began to draw me to trusting Him. He led me to various books which explained faith in God and what it means to trust. Then the scripture Philippians 4:19 became very dear to me.

"But my God shall supply **ALL** your need according to His riches in glory by Christ Jesus."

As I began to trust, probably because I was a baby Christian, our Lord met my needs quickly. It seemed that no matter what type of need I had, the Lord would meet it just when I needed it and in almost the exact way I wanted it. Our Lord's gracious kindness continued in this manner for several months as I learned to trust Jesus. My faith in His love for me grew and grew.

Suddenly, the Lord decided to change His training procedures. To my dismay, my needs were no longer being met when I wanted them. Instead, the Lord began meeting my needs in His own way. This action on the Lord's part caused me much anguish. I still felt I could trust the Lord, but the system was not working like I felt it should. I wanted my needs met when I felt

I had the need, just as babies do! Since my needs were not being met in this manner, it seemed "**TRUSTING**" by itself was not the answer to the abiding life.

At this point, the Lord picked me up, brushed me off and returned my peace and joy. This time, He began to deal with me on the power of praise. He awakened within me an understanding of the tremendous power that is unleashed as we praise God.[8] For days; I praised the Lord for everything. Gradually, however, the adverse conditions of the world began to get to me. Soon, I found myself praising God, but my joy was gone.

Shortly after my joy left, I found I could no longer praise our Lord regardless of what was happening to me. I then realized that praise in and of itself was not the total answer to living the victorious life. It seemed once again that all was confusion. If I could not trust our Lord for my needs when I felt I needed them and if praising God consistently was impossible because there was no joy in it, was my life to be lived as I had lived before I was saved?

Once again our Lord reached down and picked me up. Again, I felt His love as my peace and joy were restored. Now the Lord began to show me a third phase of Christian life… surrender. My spirit jumped immediately. I felt that this must be the key to a joyful Christian life.

I began to realize that the Lord not only wanted control of all of my possessions, my ambitions and my desires, but **He also wanted all of me!** The Lord explained surrender to me in the following way.

"Before the world was ever made, I planned your life. I planned every work I wanted my Son to do through you. I then placed in you the talent and ability necessary to do those things I planned for you to do. I drew a road map of your life and then filed it away until the time came when I could put it to use."

"My child, I waited with excitement and anticipation for the day to come when you would be born into the world. Then the day came. As you grew older, you did exactly what I knew you would do. You grabbed hold of the steering wheel of your life and took off running. You ran into this wall and then that one, always seeking your own desires, your own ambitions, and your own pleasures.

"Then my child came the glorious day when you gave up your own desires and turned your life over to Me. At that moment, you took your hands off of the steering wheel of your life and permitted Me to put my hands on it. Immediately, I took out the plan for your life and began to move you in My perfect will.

"My child, there is only room for one pair of hands on the steering wheel of your life. When you are attached to **anything**, then your hands are on the steering wheel as far as that subject is concerned. <u>**As a result, you will not hear My voice or know My perfect will for you, concerning that particular subject.**</u> When you surrender something to Me, then in My time, I can make My perfect will known to you concerning it."

<u>**My brother and sister in Christ, these words apply to every Christian.**</u> Please read them again. Our Lord is speaking directly to you.

IS SURRENDER THE KEY?

With our Lord's words ringing in my spirit, I began to surrender everything to the Lord. In the beginning, it was great! Each time I surrendered a problem, I would be released from the worry of it. Things went along great for several weeks.

Then one day, the Lord began to show me that surrender in itself was not the total answer. I would surrender a problem to the Lord and as in the past, I would be freed from the worry. But shortly, the problem and the worry would come back. It seemed that every time I tried to surrender a problem to the Lord, it would stick to me instead of staying with the Lord.

Now my Christian walk got really tough. I wanted to lead a true Christian life complete with love, joy and peace. Yet, I found I could not do it. I had tried trust, praise and surrender... one-by-one... yet, in the end, I always ended up depressed and without the fruits of the Holy Spirit.

Worse even than that, was the fact our Lord had told me to talk only about love and faith and I knew nothing about either of them.

This was the frame of mind I was in that Easter morning when our Lord quietly said, "What I mean is, you can have total faith in My love for all of your needs."

The Lord was telling me to lift my eyes to His love! I had been told to stand on the scriptures to get my needs met. Without realizing it, I had been **demanding** that God honor His words. The Lord was saying something new to me. He was saying...

"**Accept My word as true and finished!** Don't waste time standing on it and quoting it until you work up enough faith in your faith, hoping to get your need met.

"**Instead my son, let My word fill your mind and spirit. Let My word lead you to My love. Let My word prove My love. Then stand on My word, cling to My love and I will meet your need in My own time and in My own way.**"

"As you rest in My love, My fruits shall flow in you and through you like rivers of living water." (That's jumping up and down shouting news!) Our only purpose on this earth is, by the grace of God and the power of the Holy Spirit, to get in a position where the fullness of the Godhead can flow through us like a river of living water to a lost and dying world. People will see Jesus in us!

WHY CLING TO GOD'S LOVE?

Before we discuss how to cling to God's love, let's let God's word answer the question. "Why should we cling to God's love?" Let's look at Psalm 91: 14-16 and let God answer that question for us. Please notice our position is to cling to His love and acknowledge His authority by believing all things are possible.

"Because he (she) hath placed himself **to cling unto my love,** therefore I will deliver him.

"I will set him on high because **he has acknowledged my authority.**

"He shall call upon me and I will answer him.

"I will be with him in trouble.

"I will deliver him and make him great.

"With long life, I will satisfy him and show him my salvation."

*Interpretation of Psalm 91:14-16 using Strong's Hebrew Concordance.

HOW TO CLING TO GOD'S LOVE

One day as I sat reading at my desk, the Lord began to show me that my past experiences were really a schooling program that He had put me through in order that I might understand the next part of the progressive vision He was about to show me. Here is what He said to me: *__If you use S. T. P., you will run perfect forever!__*

I said, "Lord, I do not understand what You are talking about. I believe S.T.P. is some type of motor lubricant that is used in racing cars so that when the parts work real fast, there is no friction."

The Lord said, *"My S.T.P. is surrender, trust and praise. First, you **SURRENDER** the problem to Me. Then **TRUSTING** My love for all of your needs, you come to realize that I would not let anything happen to you unless it is part of My plan to mold you into My image, draw you closer to Me and, most important, lead you to a blessing.*

*As you believe this deep in your spirit, you will begin to **PRAISE**[14] and thank Me. You know I am in control of everything that is happening to you and, in the end; it shall work for your good.*[10]

Then our Lord let me know that when His children are using S.T.P., **they are abiding in Him** and His love will then automatically flow through them to other people.[11] This was the first time that it began to dawn on me that if we keep the first commandment He gave us to love and trust Him, that He would **automatically** fulfill the second commandment to love others through us… if we are willing to step out in faith to do it.

TRUTH OR DECEPTION

The words of our Lord concerning S.T.P. sounded great, but I realized the devil can also speak to me. I had to know if S.T. P. was scriptural. I then said, "Lord, if this is really you speaking to me, please prove that these words you have given me are scriptural." I had heard that the devil loves nothing better than to place Christians in bondage with pious formulas that seem to be of God… especially religious formulas and rituals.

The Lord then gave me these scriptures: Philippians 4:6-7 and 19.

4:6 ... "Be careful for nothing (don't worry about anything); but in everything by **PRAYER**, and **SUPPLICATION** with **THANKSGIVING** let your requests be made known unto God."

4:7 ... "and the Peace of God which passeth all understanding shall keep your hearts and minds through Christ Jesus."

4:19 ... "But my God shall supply all your need according to His riches in glory by Christ Jesus."

Before I close this chapter and move into the next chapter in which we will go into S.T.P. in depth, I would like to present S.T.P. to you as I see it today. First of all, it is not a formula; **it is a way of life!**

Many of us Christians are like Martha, the sister of Lazarus, who was raised from the dead. We are busy, busy trying to do something for the Lord, but complaining all the while. Many of us are complaining because the works we are doing are ours and not the Lord's. Our Lord seems to be saying that before He comes back, all Christians must become like Martha's sister, Mary. They must use S.T.P. and rest at His feet.

Our Lord promises us that from time to time, He will work a work of His Father through us that was finished from the foundation of the world.[12] Jesus wants to do the calling!

We will find by resting at our Lord's feet, that when our Lord does a work through us, more good will be accomplished in one hour than could have been done had we worked on our own all week long. We need to heed our Lord's words that He spoke to Martha. Do they apply to you... to me?

> *"Martha, Martha, thou art careful (worried) and troubled about many things, but one thing is needful; and Mary hath chosen that good part, which shall not be taken away from her." (Luke 10:41-42)*

Mary **chose** to sit at the feet of Jesus... to rest in His love... to trust His love for **all** of her needs. As we will see, resting in our Lord's love is not a life of inactivity on the **PATH**. Our work is to constantly do **"the next right thing."**

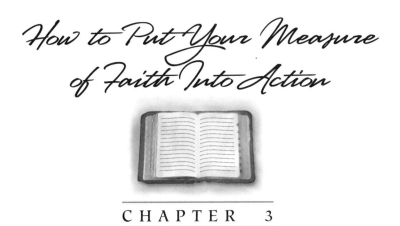

How to Put Your Measure of Faith Into Action

CHAPTER 3

Almost immediately the Lord put a real desire in my heart to use S.T.P. unceasingly all day long. More than a formula, I soon found out that only by using S.T.P. can a person **PUT HIS OR HER FAITH INTO ACTION**. When I used S.T.P., I found myself in perfect peace, sitting at the feet of Jesus. During those times, I could hear His voice really clear and His love bubbled out of me to other people. When I failed to use S.T.P., I soon lost my peace. Like Peter; I too began to sink as I took my eyes off of Jesus.

In order for you to understand how S.T.P. is backed up by the scriptures, I would like to take the scriptures the Lord gave me and let you see their relationship to S.T.P.

Philippians 4:6 ... **BE CAREFUL FOR NOTH-ING:** This means we are not to worry about anything. However, we are to do something. By **PRAYER** (trust) and **SUPPLICATION** (surrender) with **THANKS-GIVING** (praise), *let your requests be made known unto God.*

The word **PRAYER** comes from the Greek word **PROS-YOO-KHAY,** which means **"WORSHIP."** Worship is the highest form of trust! If we trust God's love for all of our needs, no matter what is happening to us, then we are giving Him worship... which leads to **PRAISE.**

The word **SUPPLICATION** means "humble plea" or "humble request" in the English language. However, when we trace its true Bible meaning back in the Greek, we find that the word supplication in the Greek is **DEH'OM-AHEE** and the verb **DEH'O** which means "to surrender one's self and requests to another's will."

The word **THANKSGIVING** is praise when it is given to God as an act of worship. Thanksgiving can only flow from a heart **that has abandoned its own desires and seeks only the will of its heavenly Father.** Thanksgiving that flows from a heart manifesting **SURRENDER** and **TRUST** believes beyond a shadow of a doubt that God is in charge of the situation and all things are working for its good according to God's purpose. **TRUE THANKSGIVING HAS NO DESIRED END IN SIGHT, BUT THE GLORY OF GOD!**

It is enough that God is in charge! Because of God's love, the abandoned heart knows that regardless of the outcome, the results will be an abundant blessing. **THIS IS FAITH IN ACTION!**

OUR LORD'S INSTRUCTION TO ME ON HOW TO PUT OUR FAITH IN ACTION

*"First, **SURRENDER** THE NEED OR PROBLEM TO Me. Be specific! Tell Me exactly what the problem is. As you surrender the problem to Me, I will see that you are willing to let go of the problem and that you want Me to handle it. Now begin to **TRUST** My love for all of your needs. Begin to think about how much I*

*love you! Your Bible is full of scriptures that prove My love for you in this situation. Begin to study these scriptures and meditate on them. **The word of My love shall renew your mind.***"

"*Soon from deep within you, shall come a knowing that I do love you and that I would never let a single thing happen to you unless it was a part of My plan to mold you, draw you closer to Me, and best of all, to lead you to a new blessing. Once you get a knowing in your spirit that Romans 8:28[10] is true and that nothing can ever happen to you without My permission, S.T.P. will become your way of life.[13] My abundant life will then flow in you and through you to others.*"

It is a must that we stay in the trust part of S.T.P. until the problem we are using S.T. P. on is no longer bigger than our faith. You will know when your faith in our Lord's love for you has grown larger than the problem because all of a sudden peace will flood your heart. **With a spirit of confident expectation toward a solution or blessing,** despite the fact the problem situation has not changed according to human conditions or sight, you should begin to thank and praise the Lord for the situation just the way it is. As you thank and praise Him and trust His love, you will feel joy rise up within you.

S.T.P. CHANGES THINGS!

1. As you **SURRENDER** the problem to the Lord, you get immediate freedom from it. This does not mean the problem immediately goes away, but it no longer bothers you. My experience has proven that if you only use surrender, you will get freedom from the problem, but it will come back and worry you.

2. As you **TRUST** God's love for all of your needs, peace will flood your heart. The trust part of

S.T.P. is the phase in which, as you meditate on the Word, your faith begins to expand. It is time we stopped standing on the scriptures and calling that faith. Faith is more than just demanding our needs be met because we find a particular scripture that will meet our need. **The purpose of the scriptures is to lead us to God's love.** If we stand on God's word and cling to His love, we shall receive abundant blessings. God can bless us, not because our faith to stand upon the scriptures is so strong, but because our faith in His love is really worship and He rewards us accordingly.

<u>It is a must that you stay in the Trust phase of S.T.P. until peace floods your being</u>. This will happen when you are so full of scriptures that prove God's love for you that you know He is in charge of the situation and leading you to a blessing.

The scripture to back up this infilling of peace is Philippians 4:7 which says: *"And the peace of God, which passeth all understanding shall keep your <u>hearts</u> and <u>minds</u> through Christ Jesus."* When you begin to experience peace, then move into praise, whether you feel like it or not.

3. As you make a cold business decision to thank and **PRAISE** God with <u>a spirit of anticipation,</u> then the power of God, which is the love of God, will flow through you into the situation and begin to heal it.

The scripture to back this up is Philippians 4:19, which says: *"But, my God shall supply all your need according to His riches in glory by Christ Jesus."*

It is important to realize that **we do not praise God for giving us the problem.** The problem did not come from God! Instead, we praise God because we know he permitted the problem, is in charge of the problem, has the solution, and is leading us to a blessing.[14-13-10]

First we surrender the situation. Then we trust by thinking on God's word. As peace comes, we make a cold business decision to trust God's love completely. We then start thanking him and praising Him, telling Him we trust His love and we believe that he is using this situation for our good. **Our foundation of trust is based on His love for us.**

As you can see, S.T.P. is a way of life. A Christian can take a problem that would normally worry him and by using S.T.P., he can actually turn the whole situation into a blessing not only for himself, but for our Lord as well. As we use S.T.P., we give the glory and honor to our Father in Heaven. The key to S.T.P. is that as we use it, **we are having total faith in our Lord's love for all of our needs. THIS IS THE HIGHEST FORM OF WORSHIP!** This is how we put our faith into action!

GOOD NEWS ON THE PATH

One day our Lord made trusting Him in the midst of a tough situation a whole lot easier. Here is what he said to me:

"Before the world was ever made, I saw every trial that would befall <u>each</u> of my children. Because I love <u>each</u> one so much, I desired to turn their mourning into dancing, to wipe their tears from their eyes."[15]

"To do this, <u>I placed a seed of abundant blessing and opportunity in the core of every trial they would</u>

endure. As My children use My S.T.P., the seed pops open and the abundant blessing begins to grow. As they trust My love, they fertilize the blessing with My word. As they praise Me and thank Me, believing with all their heart that Romans 8:28[10] is true, living water, (Holy Spirit) infuses my life into the situation and I begin to change things. In due season, My children will see the miracle working power of My revitalizing life as the abundant solution manifests itself in the fullness of My glory."[7-16]

"When My children grumble, fuss, worry and speak about the situation with the same confession the world speaks, My abundant seed lies dormant and the abundant solution is never manifested for that particular situation."

"My S.T.P. brings forth the abundant fruit of my righteousness for <u>all</u> who will use it, <u>not just to get a blessing,</u> but to give Me glory and honor in the midst of a harmful situation, **BY TRUSTING MY LOVE FOR ALL OF THEIR NEEDS."**

<u>YOUR MEASURE OF FAITH</u>

With your permission, I would like to explain the relationship of S.T.P. to faith. We know that each Christian has been given "the measure of faith.[17] However, some Christians are able to put their faith into action in a greater way and thereby, handle larger problems and receive greater blessings.

How do they do it? Whether they realize what they are doing or not, here is what they are doing. They are using their measure of faith… as small as it might be… to light a fuse, which in due season is going to cause an explosion of God's "Love" power, that is going to blow the problem right out of existence. Please let me explain.

Our measure of faith is very small. It was given to us for only one reason, to be used for one purpose. We are to use our faith to surrender, or yield a person, place, thing, situation, trial, failure, sin, etc. to Jesus.

He said over and over He could do nothing of Himself, He said we should follow Him. Therefore, knowing we can do nothing of ourself, all we can do when a problem comes up is to let go and give it to Jesus. We can only do this because we were given a measure of faith... a faith that can only get us salvation. For total restoration to the blessings God wants to give us on this earth, we need the faith of Jesus in us.

After we use our faith to surrender or yield the situation to the Lord, our tank is empty. We have run out of faith fuel. If we stop now, we will find we still have the problem.

What do we do? We go to our spiritual gas station. We start reading and meditating on the word of God. Since Jesus is the word, His presence begins to build up within us. All of a sudden, peace floods our soul. We know that we know that we know that God loves us, is in charge of the situation, and all things are working for our good according to His purpose.

Truly, Jesus was telling us a secret of the Kingdom when He said, "If you have faith small as a mustard seed, ye shall say unto this mountain, be thou removed and it shall happen.[26] The mustard seed is our measure of faith, used to activate the faith of Jesus in us.[35]

How God's Kind of Faith Grows

CHAPTER 4

Every child of God must come to know how God works. One of the most important things you need to know is how to put your measure of faith into action. Then, no matter how big the problem, your faith in God's love for all of your needs will always be large enough to handle it. In reality, when you get past surrender and move into trust, it is the expanding faith of Jesus operating in you that is having total faith in God's love for all of your needs.

Faith grows in this manner. Let's suppose our measure of faith is as big as Figure A in the Example.

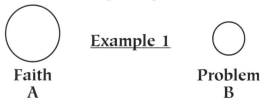

Example 1

Faith
A

Problem
B

Let us suppose a problem comes along that is as little as figure B. Since our faith is bigger than our problem, our mind and emotions will tell us that God is in charge and everything will turn out all right. We are then able to surrender the problem to our Lord Jesus, trust His love for the solution and with a peaceful heart, start praising him and really mean it. Our faith is bigger than the problem!

A word of caution: There are two kinds of faith. Faith in **your** ability to believe in God's word is really faith in your faith and is deeply rooted in pride. This type of faith will crack under extreme pressure. Its foundation is of the flesh and not of the spirit.

<u>**Faith in God's love**</u> for all of your needs is based totally on the spiritual foundation of God's word which leads you to God's love. This type of faith says, "Though you slay me, Yet will I trust you." (Job 13:15)

<u>PROBLEM IS BIGGER THAN OUR FAITH</u>

Let's suppose the problem has to do with your health. The doctor says you have cancer of the liver. You feel you have the best medical doctor possible and treatments are to begin immediately. However, tonight worry, anxiety, and fear are overwhelming you. You sit down with your Bible and concordance and begin to use S.T.P. on the situation. You say, "Lord Jesus, right now I pick up this cancer that the doctor diagnosed, and I lay it at your feet." (In your mind, picture yourself walking right up to the throne of God with this cancer in a big bushel basket and laying it at the feet of Jesus.)

You then say, "Dear Jesus, You are the great physician! You are my healer! You are in charge of my life. You are my life! I believe that You have permitted (not caused) this cancer to come on me because as I use S.T.P. on it, You are going to use it for my good according to Your purpose."[10]

At this point, you are saying the words, but fear is so strong in you that you do not know if you really believe what you are saying or not. Your eyes are fixed on the cancer instead of on God's power and love. Figure A in Example 2 is the measure of faith you have right now. Figure B is the cancer problem. So far, you are operating only on <u>your</u> measure of faith which is as small as a mustard seed.

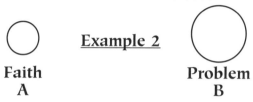

Example 2

Faith
A

Problem
B

You can see that the problem is much larger than your faith. If you permit this situation to continue, fear will continue to grow. Soon, you will believe in your heart that the very worst thing you fear is going to come upon you ... and it will! What you believe in your heart, in due season, you will speak with your mouth. This will bring the very thing you fear into reality in your life! Faith can work in a positive or negative way in our life based upon what we believe and what we say.

Matthew 12:34 says, "Out of the abundance of the heart, the mouth speaks." Proverbs 12:18 says, "The tongue of the wise is health." Proverbs 15:4 says, "A wholesome tongue is a tree of life." Proverbs 18:21 says, "Death and life are in the power of the tongue." Psalms 50:23 says, "Whoso offereth praise glorifieth Me and to him that ordereth his conversation aright will I shew the salvation of God." (Salvation, in the Hebrew translates to "liberty, deliverance, prosperity, and safety")

Please understand that as a child of God, you have the nature of God.[18] God spoke the world into existence. (Genesis Chapter 1) You and I literally speak our world into existence based upon what we believe in our heart about the situations we encounter in our life. **WE MUST SPEAK ONLY WHAT**

GOD'S WORD SAYS! Only then can God's word be fulfilled in our life. A final proof can be found in Proverbs 4:20-22.

"My child, listen to my words, incline your ear unto my sayings, Let them not depart from your eyes. Keep them in the midst of your heart. For they are life unto those who take hold of them, and health (medicine) to all of their flesh (the body)."

TOOLS FOR FAITH GROWING

We grow our faith by believing in our heart that God's words are true and by confessing these words with our tongue. To do this, we must use our Bible and a concordance. The concordance lists all of the words of the Bible. If you are using the King James Version of the Bible, you need a concordance that is based on the King James Version. If a Catholic Bible, then a Catholic concordance, etc. The concordance will help you find the scriptures you need to deal with your particular problem. For example, if we have a health problem, we would look for words like health, medicine, healing, life, etc. The concordance will show you where to find these words in your Bible. As you read these scriptures, believing them and confessing them with your tongue, your faith in God's love will expand.

OUR MEASURE OF FAITH ACTIVATES THE FAITH OF JESUS IN US!

We, who have been born again, were given a measure of faith. I have found, we can use our measure of faith for only one purpose and this is to yield or surrender something to the Lord. That's the end of our measure of faith. If we are going to get peace and if we want the abundant seed to open, we have to begin operating on the faith of Jesus. He is the word of God. As we move into the trust part of S.T.P., we begin to search the scriptures to prove God's love for us is sufficient in this situation. Each scripture brings more of the faith of Jesus into our spirit. "All things are possible to those that have the faith of Jesus flowing through them into the situation." Jesus has faith without measure ready to flow through you. Search the scriptures!

LET'S GROW OUR FAITH

Please pick one particular problem that has surfaced in your life that has been causing you worry, anxiety, and maybe fear. Pick a big one. We are going to continue with our cancer example, but, you can substitute your problem for the textbook one.

In the following example, we see the problem is bigger than our faith.

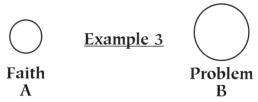

Example 3

Faith
A

Problem
B

SURRENDER ... (speak the words with your tongue) "Lord Jesus, right now, I surrender to you _____." (Name it) Picture yourself walking up to His throne and laying the problem at His feet.

TRUST ... (Speak the words with your tongue.) "Lord, I want to trust your love. Please help my unbelief. Lord, by your Holy Spirit, please show me in Your word, proof that I can have total faith in Your love for all of my needs, especially for the solution of this problem." (Name it)

Now, we take out our Bible and concordance and begin to look up scriptures that prove God is in charge of the situation and that His love will meet all of our needs. Once you begin to use S.T.P. on every area of your life, you will see the faith and fullness of the life of Jesus manifested in and through you, and you will experience true restoration.[19]

Note: God's word is true reality! It never changes! Everything else is subject to God's power and can be changed. We must pay no attention to what we hear or see, or think or feel, unless it lines up with God's word. Ask the Holy Spirit to explain God's word to you by showing you other scriptures relating to the same subject.

Below, I have listed some scriptures as an example to show you that as we think on each one, our faith in God's love will grow and grow. Take a moment and study each one looking for proof that you can have total faith in God's love for your need. Remember, trusting God's love for us means we are willing to let loose of what we want and are willing to let God do what he wants to do in the situation! Because we trust his love, we know it will work for our good!

Philippians 4:6 ... "Be careful for nothing (don't worry about anything). But in everything by prayer and supplication with thanksgiving, let your request be made known unto God."

Would God ask you to make your needs known to Him if He was not interested in helping you?

Romans 8:37 ... "Nay, in all these things we are more than conquerors through Him (Jesus) that loved us."

What did Jesus accomplish for us by His death and resurrection? He destroyed the works of the devil, of sin, sickness, poverty, and death for us! He made a way that we could be adopted into the family of God with its characteristics of Holiness, health, abundance and life. Our job is to confess our inheritance. We are <u>more</u> than conquerors.

Now that we have given our Lord the problem as He told us to do and we understand we are a child of God's and thus, "More than a Conqueror", let's fill ourselves full of scriptures that show how much God loves us. Don't just read them. Think on each one!

John 3:16 ... "For God so loved the world that He gave his only begotten Son, that <u>whosoever believeth in Him</u> should not perish, but have everlasting life."

Romans 5:8 ... "God commendeth His love toward us, in that, while we were yet sinners, Christ died for us."

Roman 5:1 ... "Therefore being justified by faith, we have peace with God through our Lord Jesus Christ."

Isaiah 53:4-5 ... "Surely He hath borne our griefs (sickness), and carried our sorrows, yet we did esteem him stricken of God and afflicted. But, He was wounded for our transgressions, He was bruised for our iniquities, the chastisement of our peace was upon him and with His stripes <u>we are healed.</u>" (H-7495 Strongs ... to cure, to heal, to repair, thoroughly make whole)

Psalm 92:12-14 ... God says, "The righteous shall flourish like the palm tree. He shall grow like a cedar in Leb'a-non. Those that be planted in the House of the Lord shall flourish in the courts of our God. They shall still bring forth fruit in old age. They shall be fat (rich and fertile) and flourishing."

Jeremiah 29:11 ... "For I know the things I think toward you, saith the Lord. Thoughts of peace and not of evil, to give you an expected end." (To give us the thing we hope for).

Psalm 41:1-3 ... "Blessed is he that instructs the oppressed. The Lord will deliver him in time of trouble. The Lord will preserve him and keep him alive and he shall be blessed upon the earth. And, thou wilt not deliver him unto the will of his enemies. The Lord will strengthen him upon the bed of sickness. Thou wilt overturn his bed of sickness."

Psalm 91:14-16 ... God says, "Because he has placed himself to cling unto my love, therefore, I will deliver him. I will set him on high because he hath acknowledged my authority. He shall call upon me and I will answer him. I will be with him in trouble. I will deliver him and make him great. With long life, I will satisfy him and show him my salvation.

Romans 8:28 ... "And we know that all things work together for good to them that love God, to them who are the called, according to His purpose.

John 10:10 ... "The thief (the devil and his demons) cometh not but for to steal and to kill and to destroy. (Jesus says) ... I am come that they might have life and that they might have it more abundantly."

As we think on these scriptures, we can know each child of God is special in God's eyes. He has so many blessings He wants to give each one of us, if we will only let loose of what we want and trust His love enough to let Him do whatever He desires to do to us, for us or through us.

If you have been really studying and thinking on the above scriptures, a miracle has happened in your life. Your faith, which began as small as a mustard seed, has begun to grow by the faith of Jesus. It may be that your faith is now bigger than the problem. If that is the case, peace has filled your heart and you

have begun thanking God for His love. This is called
the sacrifice of Praise.[20] <u>Once we have peace about
the situation, we must start praising God whether we
feel like it or not.</u>

On the other hand, if you are having a hard time
believing God's word really applies to your situation
or if you are having a real problem in letting go of the
situation and giving it to the Lord, the problem is still
bigger than your faith and you are still hurting.

At this point, you need to surrender the fact that
<u>you cannot surrender the problem totally to the Lord,
at this time.</u> You then trust His love and understanding for you just where you are.

Since all things work for your good according to
God's purpose, even now with your apparent lack of
faith, as you use S.T.P, you are on your way to wholeness. We will cover this situation in more detail later.

EVER INCREASING FAITH

 Example 4

Faith   **Problem**

A   B

Our faith started small. Notice how it expanded by
the faith of Jesus until it was larger than the problem.
As we meditated on God's word, our mind began to
believe that God really does love us. He really will
meet our need. As the mind started to believe, the
emotions began to sense God's love. These emotions
excited the will to make a decision to believe God.
Each time a decision was made, our faith expanded
as more and more of the faith of Jesus began to flow

into us. The more scriptures we mediate on, the more decisions the will makes, and the greater the increase of faith.

Any scripture that proves God loves you and proves what he did for you will make your faith grow. I have found that in the beginning, if you carry a small "Jesus Promise Book" with you, it is a great help. The scriptures are listed by topics, so you can quickly find God's promises for your needs or even for your failures. Yes, we use S.T.P. on our sins, too. It "**All**" works for our good if we trust God's saving love for "**All**" of our needs. "God's grace is sufficient for us. His strength is made perfect in our weakness". (2 Corinthians 12:9)

PRAISE

How do we know when our faith is bigger than the problem? How do we know when to move from trust to praise? Philippians 4:6-7 tells us that if we use S.T.P., then "the peace of God, which passes all understanding, shall keep your hearts and minds by Christ Jesus." You will know immediately when your faith has grown larger than the problem.

Peace will flood your soul. As you begin to thank God, praise will begin to bubble out of you. You will get excited! You will have the victory in Christ Jesus, although the appearance of the problem has not changed one bit.

Isaiah 26:3 says, "Thou (our Lord) wilt keep him in perfect peace whose mind is stayed on Thee, because he trusteth in Thee."

FAITH FACTS

1. Do not move out of the trust phase until peace floods your heart. The bigger the problem, the more meditation in the scriptures it will take for you to get the victory.

2. Remember this: Our Lord wants to solve your problems, but He can not do so until you are <u>willing to die to what you want</u> and willing to thank Him and praise Him for the situation just the way it is, <u>believing His love is sufficient for you.</u> He permitted it, so we can trust him to use it for our good.

3. The final healing power for any problem will only begin to flow as we give praise with a joyful heart <u>full of anticipation</u> for a blessing. Only then can God's healing power flow through us to the problem

4. After you use S.T.P. on a problem, if you have used the Word of God faithfully, you will be all aglow and the concern for the problem will have disappeared in your bubbles of praise. Later, the problem may come back to your mind. If this happens, you do not have to use S.T.P. on it again.

You already have the victory! In your spirit, just look up to the Lord and say, "Lord, I thank you and praise you for everything you are doing on that problem." Then keep on praising Him. As soon as the devil realizes that every time he brings a problem to your mind, you start praising God, he will stop bringing up problems.

5. <u>At times, a problem will come up that you are so attached to that you just cannot surrender it.</u> When this occurs, you will know it. You will surrender the problem to the Lord, try to move

into trust, and find you just can't trust. The reason is: <u>deep in your heart, you just do not want to submit your will to the Lord's will on this matter.</u> When this occurs, don't feel bad about it. Here is what you do.

<u>Surrender the fact to the Lord that you cannot surrender this problem.</u> Say, "Lord, I surrender the fact that I cannot surrender this problem to You (name it). I trust Your love for me. I know You love me so much that You understand why I cannot surrender it. <u>Lord, I **will** to surrender it.</u> You will have to come and take it from me. Lord, You love me so much. I just thank You for everything that is happening in my life.

At this point, I now find I can surrender the first thing. It seems as I began to praise God, my will becomes willing to come in line with our Lord's will. Don't try to understand all that I am saying just by reading. You need S.T.P. experience. The Holy Spirit will guide you. His job is to lead us into all truth.

6. This is one of the most important things I can tell you about S.T.P. It is a must that you name the **specific** thing you are surrendering. It is no good to say, "I am surrendering all of my problems to you." You must be specific and surrender each one by name. Then, move into the trust and praise phase for that specific problem. Only then will you get victory over that specific problem.

When S.T.P. Will Not Work

CHAPTER 5

At times, I have found myself so overwhelmed with the tasks ahead of me, the failures behind me and the seemingly hopelessness of the present situation facing me, that I not only lose my peace and joy, but the weight of the burden almost become too much to bear mentally and emotionally.

When this happens, I find myself unable to single out any specific problem that is the main one. Thus, I do not know what to surrender to the Lord or even to tell Him what I cannot surrender. It seems like one big ball of trouble about to run over me. In reality, it is a confusing, overwhelming lie of the devil that God is permitting, to lead me to another blessing. Here is how the Lord showed me to handle this situation.

One morning, I woke up in this overwhelming fog. I tried to pray, but was making little headway as my mind raced to and fro among the circumstances surrounding me. Suddenly, the Lord spoke to me and said, *"Walk around the room with your arms raised. Praise me and thank me for <u>everything</u> I have done for you whether you feel like it or not. (This is a garment of praise for a spirit of heaviness). (Isaiah 61:3)*

I did what the Lord said, although I did not feel like it at all. I praised God for 15 minutes or more, and then I went in to read the Bible. I still did not feel a lot different. I still was overwhelmed with the tasks that lie ahead of me.

However, something happened when I got in the shower. All of a sudden, I started singing praises to God. They just bubbled out. The discouragement and depression left. The Holy Spirit had put a song in my heart and praise on my lips. I had learned a new lesson!

When all is confusion and discouragement and I can not point out the exact cause, I can use praise to blow a giant hole in the enemy's attack against me. Praise will do it every time!

HOW TO SEEK GOD'S FACE

Find a place where you can praise the Lord out loud. Then just start thanking Him and praising Him for all the blessings He has given you ... spiritual, mental, emotional, financial, social (relationships) and physical. At times, lift your hands above your head in total surrender to the God who loves you, saved you and is in the process of restoring you.

Walk a few feet, stop and begin to praise Him some more. Walk a few more feet, stop and talk to your Father in Heaven. Just tell Him your concerns. Walk a few more feet and sing a blessing song to our Lord. Any language that blesses the Lord is just fine!

Keep your praise simple! Praise Him for His tremendous love. Praise Him for His plan of salvation and restoration. Praise Him for Jesus and the Holy Spirit. Thank God for your family, your job, etc.

The chances are, if you are like me, you will not feel like doing this when you first start out. I found I had to make a cold business decision to praise and thank God whether I felt like it or not. Guess what? It will not be long after you get started that God will start putting the "want to" in your heart. Don't be surprised if He begins to talk to you in a small voice on the inside. Our Lord loves praise and worship from His children.

While I am praising Him, because I <u>KNOW</u> God has planted a seed of abundant blessing and opportunity in every failure, problem, situation and circumstance in my life and my family's life, I begin to thank Him for everything that looks negative in my past, present and future <u>whether I feel like it or not.</u>

My act of <u>surrendering</u> by raising my hands is an act recognized worldwide as an act of submission. My willingness to praise when everything seems to be against me, when every feeling is total discouragement, is really the highest form of <u>trust</u> in God's love. I have found that as I <u>praise</u> God in the midst of the battle, it stops the enemy dead in his tracks.

Each word of praise forces him backward until he no longer can oppress my mind, my emotions or my will. Praise God, you will have the same results! Like Moses, as you hold your hands high with Praise, your enemies of darkness will be defeated.[21] S.T.P. is the most powerful weapon man can use on earth or in the heavens. <u>God wonders why it is so seldom used.</u>

SPEAK S.T.P. WITH YOUR TONGUE

When you use S.T.P., it is a **must** that you speak the words <u>with your tongue</u>. It is **not** enough to think them in your mind. I went through a long period of using S.T.P. on problems and doing it only in my mind. I could not understand what was wrong. Although I was using S.T.P., I was not getting freed from the problem. Most importantly, peace was not flooding my inner being and praise was not bubbling out of me.

Then one day I heard a Christian brother talking about the fact that what we believe in our heart (mind, emotions and will) and confess with our mouth, we receive.[22] This reminded me of Romans 10:9-10. "That if thou shalt confess with thy mouth, the Lord Jesus and shalt believe in thine heart that God hath raised him from the dead, thou shalt be saved. For with the heart (mind, emotions, will) man believeth unto righteousness and <u>with the mouth, confession is made unto salvation</u>".

I had **not** been confessing S.T.P. with my tongue. I had been thinking S.T.P. with my mind. In the beginning, the Lord had me actually lift my hands as if I was handing Him the problem as I verbally surrendered the problem to Him. I then spoke out loud the fact that I trusted His love as I reminded Him of His word. I then moved into verbal praise. Somewhere along the line I lapsed into mental S.T.P. and lost the power to make my faith grow. Don't let this happen to you!

If possible, go into a room or any place by yourself and use S.T.P. out loud. Speak the words with confidence and you shall feel your faith grow on the inside of you. If you cannot speak out loud, then speak the words softly to yourself. The key is to SPEAK the words and not just think them. God spoke the world into existence. When you speak S.T.P., you actually speak wholeness, health and prosperity into the situation, by the faith of Jesus.

You see, S.T.P. is nothing more than a way of life our Lord has given us to get the victory over our problems. It involves giving Him the problem, trusting His love then praising Him as peace and joy flood our soul. To just mumble the words of S.T.P. will do nothing for us. Used properly, our faith will always be bigger than our problems.

A Time of Patience

CHAPTER 6

One day the Lord asked me, *"Why do you think when I put The S.T.P. scriptures together, Philippians 4:6-7 and 19, that I did not just make verse 19 verse 8 instead. Then, it would have been 4:6-8."* I told the Lord I did not know why. I asked Him to tell me. Here is what He said.

"For a maturing Christian there is always a time of patience between the time a Christian uses S.T.P. and when the problem is actually resolved in the natural realm. The distance between verse 7 and verse 19 represents a time of patience that every Christian should expect to go through"[13]

Then the Lord asked me another question, *"What is a Christian supposed to do during this period of patience after he has used S.T.P. on the problem?"* I asked Him to please tell me. This is what He said: *"Look at verse 8."* I looked and here is what it said:

"Finally brethren, whatsoever things are true, whatsoever things are honest, whatsoever things are pure, Whatsoever things are just, whatsoever things are of good report, if there be any virtue and if there be any praise, think on these things." (Philippians 4:8)

In essence, the Lord was saying, *Use S.T.P., then rest
in My love. Meditate on the Word day and night and
you shall be like a tree planted by the rivers of living
water. You shall bear fruits in **My** season. Your leaf
shall never wither, and everything that you do shall
prosper* (Psalms 1:2-3).

In order to believe God's word and what it says
about you, I suggest you take a minute, bend over,
unscrew the top of your head and shake out all of the
<u>untruths</u> you have ever heard or believed about
yourself. God's word says if you are a child of God,
then you are <u>PERFECT</u> in Jesus.[23]

God sees you perfect! He sees you as a mature
Christian. The problem is, maybe <u>you do not see
yourself that way.</u>

By God's grace and our belief in His word, the
body of Christ will come to see ourselves as he sees
us. This will release the fullness of the life of Jesus in
us to others.[24]

UNFORGIVENESS VOIDS S.T.P.

<u>A reminder to all of us in Jesus's own words,</u> *"And
when ye stand praying, forgive, if you have ought
(anything) against any. That your Father also which is
in heaven, may forgive you your trespasses. But, if ye do
not forgive, neither will your Father which is in heaven,
forgive your trespasses"* (Mark 11:25-26)

*How S.T.P. Affects Us...
And God*

CHAPTER 7

In order to understand the importance of using S.T.P. in your Christian life, you must remember that S.T.P. is how we put our faith into action. The scriptures say that without faith we cannot please God.[25] Our Lord says if we have faith the size of a mustard seed, we can say to a problem, "Be gone!," and it will be gone.[26] Over and over the Word of God tells us that the Christian life is a life of faith.[27]

But wait...James 2:17 says, "FAITH IF IT HATH NOT WORKS IS DEAD". There seems to be a conflict only if you do not truly understand how faith works. The scriptures tell us very clearly that we are to rest at the feet of Jesus, cease our own works,[28] and let the love of God flow through us to other people. We rest at the feet of Jesus, that is, we abide in Him and He in us when we are in an attitude of total worship, which comes about only as we use S.T.P. As we rest at the feet of Jesus, His love begins to flow through us to other people. <u>This love will be manifested through us as works of unselfish love to others.</u>

As we rest at the feet of Jesus, we can hear him clearly. (HE SPEAKS TO US IN MANY DIFFERENT WAYS.) From time to time, we will feel he wants us to do something for Him. It may seem impossible, but we must be obedient. We will find as we lift our foot to take a step in the direction of doing the impossible task, that even before our foot hits the floor, our Lord has already gone before us to make the way. He gave us no indication He would help us accomplish the task until we not only made a decision to be obedient, but we actually stepped out in faith to do it.

The task that He gave us to do is one of our Father's works that our Lord Jesus Christ is doing through us.[9] Thus, faith without works is dead! It is impossible to have faith in God's love for our needs and not have God's love and works flowing through us to others. Anything we do big or small that is a blessing to another person is a work of God through us. Look for an opportunity to be a blessing to others. Start at home! Start today!

RESTING IN GOD'S LOVE

Let's look at the position of resting at our Lord's feet or resting in His love. What do we mean by the words, **"resting in His love?"** By these words, we mean that no matter what is happening to us, based on God's Word, we believe our Lord is in control of the situation and all things are working for our good according to His purpose. Let me make one thing clear. Resting in His love does not mean we lay in bed all day waiting on the Lord to tell us to get up and do something. There are certain things that every human being in this world has to do every day. Therefore, a Christian should get up each morning and do those things in a normal way unless the Lord intervenes in his schedule. "DO THE NEXT RIGHT THING You FEEL IN YOUR HEART YOU SHOULD DO!"

We should get up in the morning and lay everything we are and have at our Lord's feet. This includes our time and where we are to go that day and what we are to do. We let the Lord know that he is our top priority! By using S.T.P. on our life and schedule, we remove our hands from the steering wheel of our life and we are able to hear the Lord when he needs to change our plans in the middle of the day. All day long, we rest at His feet as we go about our normal day's work. We know when we are resting at His feet because His love is bubbling out of us to other people.

If at anytime during the day, we selfishly become attached to a desire, idea or anything, at that moment our hands go back on the steering wheel of our life. The Lord's hands come off. Our joy stops. His love stops bubbling out of us and soon we are out of His perfect will. All we have to do is realize the situation, repent, use S.T.P. on the matter, and we are back at the feet of Jesus. Praise God for His love!

Let's suppose we need a job. We have heard we should pray and the Lord has a perfect job for us. As a result, we are afraid to go out and look for a job because we might get the wrong one. Instead, we do nothing waiting for God to bring the job to us. Is this inaction God's perfect will for us? The answer is no! We are to use S.T.P. and surrender to the Lord the fact we do not have a job. We let Him know we trust His love. We tell Him we believe that He loves us so much that if He wanted us to have a job right now we would have one. We stay in the trust phase and study the scriptures until we know He is in charge of our life and he only wants the best for us. Now we praise Him because He is Lord, because He loves us and because he has permitted this situation to work out for our good.

Since we have our hands off the situation and our Lord has His hands on it, **we are free to do some-**

thing. What do we do? We do the next right thing! We go out and look for a job.

When you live your life like this in all things...YOU ARE RESTING IN GOD'S LOVE and your needs will be met ... abundantly in God's time.

NEEDS MET

Now let's talk about getting our needs met. First, you must realize that there are two kinds of solutions to needs. One solution just meets the need. The other solution meets the need abundantly. Our Lord gave us three proofs that He desires to meet our needs abundantly ... **in this world.** He then shows us why He is unable to bestow the abundant life on many of His children.

One day the Lord spoke to me and said, *"Do you know why I have come into this world?"* I said "Lord, please tell me why." *"I have come that all might have life and have it more abundantly ... through faith ... total faith in My love for all their needs"* (John 10:10)

Our Lord explained His statement like this. First, He said He has come that all might have life. By life, He means that all might be saved and have eternal life with Him. This eternal life does not begin at physical death, but begins at the moment we have faith in Him. Moreover, this eternal life does not just mean spiritual life, but physical, mental, emotional, financial, social and verbal life as well.[29] Thus our Lord was saying that as we have faith in His Word and trust in His love and are <u>willing</u> to reach out to be a blessing to others, we will get our needs met Period, no matter what they are ... **in His time and in His way.**[7] GOD IS NOT A MAN THAT HE SHOULD LIE. (Numbers 23:19)

MISSING OUR INHERITANCE

The Lord showed me that most Christians stop in their Christian walk right at the point where our Lord came that they might have life. Few Christians move into the realm where our Lord meets their needs more abundantly (more than is needed) right on this earth. This abundance is our inheritance as Children of God as promised in God's Word. Most of God's children trust Him only for their eternal salvation, few trust His love for total restoration right on this earth.[19]

Let's look at this abundant realm. Our Lord said we get there ... THROUGH FAITH ... TOTAL FAITH IN HIS LOVE FOR ALL OF OUR NEEDS. What is this abundant realm? It is abundant life! What is abundant life? Our Lord says it is salvation, health, prosperity, and wholeness. The wholeness is spiritual, physical, emotional, financial, social, verbal and mental and in a degree that is abundant ... more than needed.[31]

Our Lord is saying that He has already planned to meet all of our needs in a manner that will give us more than we need in every area of our life.[7]

Now the question is ... "If every Christian can have surplus, why don't they get it?" The answer is two-fold. First, every child of God does not realize he is to have the abundant life. Second, if he knows he is supposed to have the abundant life, he does not know how to get it. In our Lord's statement above, He is telling us exactly how to get the abundant life ... through faith ... total faith in His love for all of our needs <u>by believing and speaking what God's Words says.</u>

How did our Lord say we show total faith in His love for all of our needs? He said we do it when we use S.T.P. By using S.T.P., we put our faith into action to activate the faith of Jesus by His word. As we put our faith into action, our faith expands and grows larger. We then CAN have total faith in His Love for all of our needs. AS WE HAVE FAITH ... HE WILL BE FAITHFUL! HE WILL MEET OUR NEED IN HIS TIME AND WAY ... ABUNDANTLY!

Our Lord said Philippians 4:6-7 and 19 were the scriptures to support S.T.P. We know verses 6 and 7 deal with surrender, trust and praise, as well as the promise of peace and joy. Let's look at verse 19. It says, *"But My God shall supply all your need according to His riches in glory by Christ Jesus."* My friend, this scripture is the first proof that I wish to offer to show you that our precious Lord desires to meet your need abundantly.

The second proof I wish to offer you lies in 3 John 2 ... *"Beloved, I wish above all things that thou mayest prosper, and be in health, even as thy soul prospereth."* If the Lord wishes me to be in good health and prosper as my soul prospers, then I need to know several things. First, what does my soul consist of? Second what makes my soul prosper? If I can make my soul prosper, then good health and prosperity will move from the spiritual realm into the natural or physical realm. (The word prosper comes from the Greek word "YOU-OD-O" which means to succeed in business affairs). (Can be spiritual or physical business affairs.)

I know what my soul consists of. It is made up of three parts... my mind, my emotions, and my will. Now the question is what can I do to make the three parts of my soul prosper? I had no idea and then one day the Lord supplied the answer. *"As you surrender to Me, your will, which is your decision-making facility, it begins to prosper. As your will becomes My will, your will prospers."* Then He said, *"As you trust My love for all of your needs, your mind begins to prosper. As you meditate in My word, your mind visualizes My love and it begins to prosper."* Last he said, *"As peace floods your soul, you begin to move into the praise part of S.T.P.,knowing I am molding you and leading you to a blessing. As a result, you get excited, and at that point, your emotions begin to prosper."*

Think about it! Our Lord is saying that every time we use S.T.P. properly, our mind, emotions and will begin to prosper. Our Lord in 3 John 2 has already promised that as our soul prospers, so shall we. Praise God, He is good! The Lord has shown me that it is a cause and effect situation. We may use S.T.P. for a while without any visual results. However, as sure as day follows night, the abundant life will follow S.T.P. if it is used unceasingly to the best of our ability.

Remember S.T.P. is not a "name it and claim it" action. <u>It is a dying to what we want! S.T.P. is an acceptance of what God is permitting in our life and a belief that it is working for our good.</u> Please read this paragraph over and over until you understand it well.

The third proof that our Lord desires to give us the abundant life is contained in Ephesians 3:20, "NOW UNTO HIM THAT IS ABLE TO DO EXCEEDINGLY, ABUNDANTLY ABOVE ALL THAT WE ASK OR THINK, ACCORDING TO THE POWER THAT WORKETH IN US."

Please notice what this scripture says. God **is able** to do for us exceedingly abundantly more than we could ever ask or think. Think about it! He is able to meet our need beyond our wildest dreams. Do you believe it? Sure you do! It's the Word of God! Then why isn't that happening in many of our lives? The answer lies in the rest of the scripture. It says our God can do **all**, <u>but **only** according to the **Power** that works within us.</u>

Praise God! This means, "The Power that works within us" is the key to whether or not we receive the exceeding abundant life. Now the question is what is the power that seems to control God's ability to fulfill our needs abundantly? I asked the Lord about this power and finally He spoke to me and said, *"This power is love and faith. The very same things I have told you to tell people about."*

Wow! Praise God! The scripture means my God is able to do exceedingly abundantly above all that we ask or think according to the power of Love and Faith that works within us. In essence, this scripture says that my God is ready and willing to give us more blessings than we could ever imagine, but the amount of blessings He is actually able to give us, <u>is in direct proportion to the amount of Faith we have in His Love for all of our needs.</u> STP is truly the pathway to the heart of God.

How to Receive the Abundant Life

CHAPTER 8

We literally limit the Holy Spirit's ability to manifest the abundance of God's nature in our life by failing to have total faith in God's Love for all of our needs.

You see, before the world was ever made, our Lord planned our life. He also planned every abundant solution to our every problem. Then when Jesus died on the cross, rose from the dead and sat at the right hand of the Father, the Father gave Jesus the complete plan for our life with its problems and abundant solutions. The key point to understand is that the solution to our every problem is already complete in Jesus! All a child of God has to do is use S.T.P. and rest at the feet of Jesus. In due season the abundant solution **has to become reality.**[7]

Our Lord gave me a visual picture of how the power of love and faith really works within each of His children. First, He said when we gave our life to Him, He came to live in our heart. At that time, He brought with him every abundant blessing to fulfill every need we would ever have for all eternity. These blessing are all wrapped up in what we call **His Love.** Our Lord said, *"Picture My love as a keg of dynamite within you. Now, picture a long fuse coming out of the* *dynamite. Now picture a match standing upright under the fuse."* Here is how I saw it.

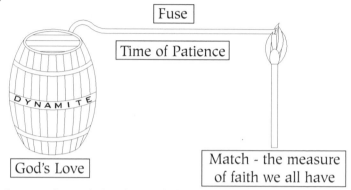

The Lord said the keg of dynamite was His Love and in it were the solutions to **all** of my problems in **abundant form.** The fuse was "a time of patience". Patience is the ability to trust the Lord constantly while under trial. The match was the measure of faith we all have.[17] The Lord said that many Christians live and die without ever once lighting the fuse and setting off the keg of dynamite which represents their abundant blessing coming into the natural realm.

To receive the abundant life, YOU MUST DIE TO SELF so that the fullness of the abundant life of Jesus becomes your life. We die to self when we make a decision to trust God's Word and his love and confess it, rather than believe what the world, the flesh and the devil is telling us.

HOW TO LIGHT THE FUSE

Here is the way the Lord showed me how you receive the Abundant Life. When a need, failure, problem or trial comes along, the first thing you must do is put your faith into action. As you put your faith into action, the match will light and the fuse will start burning. How do we put our faith into action? Use S.T.P.!

As you surrender the problem, trust God's love for everything that is happening to you and begin to praise God ...God's power, which is His love will begin to change it. Our faith is now in action. The match, which is our faith, lit the fuse and it is now burning toward the keg of dynamite.

Let's talk about the fuse. As the Lord told me, the fuse is patience, which is our ability to trust our Lord constantly while under trial. Let's go back to Philippians 4:6-7 and 19. Remember the Lord said He put verse 19 where he put it, instead of making it verse 8, because He wanted us to know there would be a time of patience between the time we used S.T.P. and when we receive the promise. Remember, also, He told us what to do in verse 8 while we were in this period of patience. MEDITATE ON THE WORD! THINK OF GOD'S LOVE! Let's look at the waiting or patience period that comes between the time we have lit the fuse and we receive the solution to our need.

First of all, since everything comes to us from the Lord by faith, it is a must that we stay in the faith realm. Once we light the match which lights the fuse, the fuse must keep burning. Did you know that the Lord told me that most Christians never receive their blessings **because their fuse goes out?** Let me give you an example.

When a problem comes along, they give it to the Lord in their own way, and this lights the fuse. Then, the period of patience sets in. After a while, since God does not take care of the problem in the time frame they have allotted Him, they try to work out a solution themselves. Now they have no testimony and they honestly do not know if God would have met their need or not. What happened? The Lord explained it this way:

"When the person started to work out the solution himself or when he began to complain about the situation or how I am handling it, he moved from the faith realm to the natural realm. When this happened, the fuse, which is patience, stopped burning toward the keg of the dynamite. <u>When the person stopped trusting My love for his need</u>, then the fuse, which is the constant trusting of Me while under trial, went out.[25]

With the fuse out, the abundant solution that is in the keg of dynamite will never explode or come into reality in the person's life. Thus many Christians have died without ever realizing the wonderful blessings that were within them, ready to be brought forth by the use of their faith.[30]

The Lord said, "Should a person move from faith into personal works or complaining and then repent, the fuse would relight." <u>It seems each blessing or solution to a problem has its own fuse length.</u> Sometimes the blessing will appear minutes after the fuse is lit. At other times, years go by before the fuse burns down and sets off the keg of dynamite, which is God's love and the blessing becomes a reality in the person's life.

The thing to remember is this. Once you light the fuse by using S.T.P., which puts your faith into action, <u>you can know</u> that sooner or later <u>if you stay in the faith realm</u>, your need will be met in an exceedingly abundant way, <u>far beyond anything you could ask or think</u>. We stay in the faith realm by thanking and praising the Lord for the situation just the way it is ... because it is working for our good according to God's purpose.

The Father's Love

CHAPTER 9

One day The Lord Jesus gave me insight into the heart of the Father by telling me what happens in heaven when a child of God uses S.T.P. Here is what Jesus said:

"My child, do you not realize how excited and full of love my Father becomes when He sees one of His children using S.T.P. on a problem? When a child of God is hit with a tremendous problem, the devil says the case is hopeless. Every human sense says the case is lost. Yet, the child of God surrenders the problem to my Father in heaven, then he begins to trust my Father's love. He searches the scriptures, receiving proof over and over again that my Father would not let a single thing happen to any of His children unless it was part of His overall plan to mold the individual and draw him to a new blessing. Despite the fact the child of God feels like he is perishing, he holds on to my Father's love and begins to praise Him and thank Him because he knows my Father is in control of the situation and it will come out all right".

"As my Father in heaven sees His child trust His love, His heart breaks for the individual. He wants to hold the child in His arms and kiss his tears away. Since the child of God has proven he will hold on to the

love of the Father no matter what happens, quickly my Father in heaven says, 'enough' to the situation".

"He reaches down, picks up the individual, wipes his tears away, sets him on a mountain and gives him the blessing. The trial hurt my Father more than it hurt the individual, yet the trial was a must because only through it can my children be molded to my image. Many of my children say "I love you", but they do not know the true meaning of the words. <u>To love Me, you must really trust Me in all things</u>. The true love of my children is proven when they use S.T.P. in all situations."

As the Lord spoke the above words, he brought to my mind that when we see Jesus, we see the Father. He said He only does what He has seen the Father do. Then He reminded me of how His heart broke when He observed the blind faith of Martha, Mary and the Jews when Lazarus died.

John Chapter 11 starting with verse 21 says, When Martha came out to meet Jesus, she said, *"Lord, if thou hadst been here my brother had not died."* Then Mary came out, fell to her knees and said the same thing. Then in verse 33, it says when Jesus saw Martha and Mary weeping and the Jews also ... HE GROANED IN HIS SPIRIT AND WAS TROUBLED. Then Jesus asked, *"Where have you laid him?"* Although they knew He could have saved Lazarus if He had wanted to, they did not get mad, but humbly said... Come and see. JESUS WEPT! Later others said, *"Could not this man which opened the eyes of the blind have caused that even this man should have not died?"* At that point Jesus again groaned within Himself.

Now the question is ... why was Jesus groaning or hurting within Himself? Why did He weep? Was it because Lazarus died? No! We can know this was not the reason because in John 11:4 Jesus said clearly, *"This sickness is not unto death, but for the glory of God, that the Son of God might be glorified thereby."* This scripture proves He was not troubled because of Lazarus' death, so why was He troubled? *"My child let me tell you why I was troubled. You see, I knew that this entire trial for Martha, Mary and the Jews was to give My Father glory and honor. When I saw Martha and Mary using S.T.P. ... trusting in My love and My Father's love in the midst of their grief, it was more than my human body could stand. I loved them so much as they accepted the fact that in their mind I had let their brother die because I did not come sooner. Yet, My child, do you realize the blessing they received in the end because of using S.T.P.?"*

"I want you to know this! Neither My Father nor I can watch one of Our children using S.T.P. in the middle of a trial without groaning in the spirit. We love so much! Although the trial is a must in order that the child be molded like Us, yet if the child of God will use S.T.P., the trial will pass quickly and My Father and I will open the windows of heaven and pour out a blessing on Our child that he will not hardly be able to believe."

I again emphasize that self-effort is not the way. SURRENDER, TRUST and PRAISE will take our hands off of the steering wheel of our life and permit the Lord to put His hands on it. <u>Faith in God's love for all of our needs is the key to not only the abundant life (having more of everything than is needed), but it is also the key to the victorious life (which is a life free from the voluntary sins of the flesh).</u> We must concentrate on the love of our Father! We must ask Him daily to reveal a deeper and deeper understanding of how much He really loves us. Remember what our Lord said, *"My yoke is easy, my burden is light!"*

Trials and problems will come. That is how we are molded from within. But for all who use S.T.P. properly ... their yoke is easy and their burden is light.

S.T.P. SCRIPTURES

EPHESIANS 5:20 ... *Giving thanks always FOR ALL THINGS unto God and the Father in the Name of our Lord Jesus Christ.*

I THESS 5:16-18 ... *Rejoice evermore, pray without ceasing. In everything give thanks, for this is the will of God in Christ Jesus concerning you.*

HEBREWS 10:35-36 ... *Cast not away therefore your confidence, which hath great recompense of reward. For ye have need of patience, that after ye have done the Will of God, ye might receive the promise.*

HEBREWS 6:12 ... *That ye not be slothful, but followers of them who through faith and patience inherit the promises.* (Notice it does not call those who do not work slothful, but instead, those who fail to wait in faith and patience.) What a Revelation!

JAMES 1:2-4... *My brethren, count it all joy when you fall into diverse temptations; knowing this, that the trying of your faith worketh patience. But let patience have her perfect work, that ye may be perfect and entire, wanting nothing.* (Patience will have her perfect work as the fuse burns. When the fuse hits God's Love — you will want for nothing!)

NOTE: The word *entire* is used only one time in the Bible. In the Greek, it comes from two Greek words. One means inheritance, patrimony. The other means complete in extent, amount, time...all, every whit, throughout whole. The word entire in the Greek means "complete in every part, perfectly sound in body through inheritance or patrimony." God's Word says we can be perfectly whole on this earth because we have been adopted into the family of God. [36] Can you believe it?

HOW GOD'S LOVE FLOWS THROUGH YOU TO A LOST AND DYING WORLD

One day some years ago, the Lord let me see myself as a beautiful shiny stainless steel pipe. It was about 24 inches around and the length was five or six feet. As I looked at it, I saw pure clean water flowing into the end of it. Looking to the other end of the pipe, muddy water was coming out.

Going over to the end that the pure water was flowing into, I looked inside of the pipe. Although the outside of the pipe was a beautiful shiny stainless steel, the inside of the pipe had clumps of mud stuck all over the sides. Now I understood why the pure clear water flowing into the pipe, came out the other end so muddy.

At this point, the Lord began to tell me what I was seeing. He explained that each one of His children are like perfect beautiful stainless steel pipes, through which the living water of the Holy Spirit wants to manifest the restoring life of Jesus to a lost and dying World.

However, there is a problem. God's "Pipes" are so full of clumps of mud, that the pure life of Jesus that flows in one end comes out of the other end so muddy that the people can not see Jesus. Our Lord showed me that the muddy clumps are the unbelief, self-centeredness and selfishness plus the man made theology and doctrines of fellowship that have drawn His children away from simply trusting His love and letting His love flow through them to others.[32]

The Lord made it clear to me that only S.T.P. will remove this filth, permitting the pure water of the Holy Spirit to flow to a thirsty and dying world.

My prayer (and I hope yours will be also) ... "Lord, bless me and bless me and bless me! Enlarge my pipe! Pour out your love and burn me out so there is nothing left, but just you. Give me the grace to die to self so that the fullness of your love and desires can flow through me to others. Keep me from evil and error. Bless me with your life, that more and more people will see Jesus through me. Amen.

C H A P T E R   1 0

The following are daily readings from a book titled *God Calling* by A.J. Russell, published by Barbour and Company Inc. These daily readings were recorded by two ladies in England as thoughts they feel very strongly they have received from the Lord. The book is a classic and many of the thoughts give us an insight into God's love. (Published by arrangement with Dodd, Mead & Company, Inc.)

November 7th … ..SELF KILLS POWER

Dwelling with Me, desiring only My Will and to do My work, My Spirit cannot fail to pass through the channel of your life into the lives of others.

Many think it is humility to say they do little, and are of little value to My world. To think *that* is pride.

What if the pipe were to say "I do so little, I wish I could be more use." The reply would be "It is not you, but the water that passes through you, that saves and blesses. All you have to do is to see there is nothing to block the way so that the water cannot flow through."

The only block there can be in *your* channel is self. Keep that out, and know that My Spirit is flowing through. Therefore all must be the better for coming in contact with both of you, because you are channels.

See this, and you will think it natural to know they are being helped, not by you, but by My Spirit flowing through you as a channel.

April 17th ... THE TWO JOYS

"My children I came. Hearts eager to do My Will send out a call that ever I find irresistible. I know no barrier then.

Resignation to My Will keeps me barred out from more hearts then does unbelief. Can anything be such a crime against Love as being resigned? My Will should be welcome with a glad wonder if I am to do my work in the heart and life.

The only resignation that could possibly be acceptable to Me is when self, ousted by my claims, accepts the inevitable and resigns the throne for Me leaving My Disciple free to carry out My Will, to welcome My Will gladly, rapturously.

In all true discipleship, and in the true spiritual development of each disciple, there is first the wonder and the joy of first acquaintance, then comes the long plain stretch of lesson learning and discipline, when joy seems so much a thing of the past as never to be recaptured again.

But, the constant experience of Me, the constant persistent recognition of My Work in daily happenings ... the ever accumulating weight of evidence in support of my guidance ... the numberless instances in which seeming chance or wonderful coincidence can be, must be, traced back to my loving forethought, ... all these gradually engender a feeling of wonder, certainty, gratitude, followed in time by Joy.

Joy is of two Kinds. The Joy born of Love and Wonder, and the Joy born of Love and knowledge, and between the experience of the two Joys lie discipline, disappointment, almost disillusion.

But, combat these in My Strength, or rather <u>cling blindly, helplessly to Me</u> and let Me combat them, persevere in obeying My Will, accept My discipline, and the second Joy will follow.

And of this second Joy it was that I said "Your Joy no man taketh from you".

Do not regret the first, the second is the greatest gift."

(Using S.T.P., in due season, you will receive the second joy that will not be taken from you.)

LOVE AND FAITH

Jesus is now combining His teachings of Love and Faith for his children. The results will be seen world wide as the miraculous power of the Holy Spirit manifesting the life of Jesus will flow through us as rivers of living water to a lost and dying world.

1. A few years ago, God's Faith teachers taught us the importance of believing and confessing God's Word as true and done.

2. Now our Lord through the Holy Spirit is teaching us the only way to really love Him is to prove our Love by using Surrender, Trust and Praise. Only then can His love flow through us to others.

3. Nothing that comes to us can defile us ... neither the world, the flesh or the devil and his demons with their fruits of sin, sickness, poverty and death ... as long as we use S.T.P. on it and confess what God's word says about our deliverance and freedom in Jesus.

4. Love by itself or faith by itself will not work. This is why many of God's children become disillusioned with the faith message. Not looking to God's love, many used the faith message to

try to get what they wanted rather than to put themselves in a position for God to do what He wanted. Instead of using the faith message as it was taught, many turned it into a name it, claim it formula for prosperity. They found this did not work! God's word is proof that love and faith must be used together.

5. 1 JOHN 3:21-24.... "Beloved, if our heart condemns us not, then have we confidence toward God and whatsoever we ask, we receive of Him, because we keep his commandments, and do those things that are pleasing in His sight. And this is His commandment. That we should believe on the name of His Son Jesus Christ and Love one another as he gave us commandment." And he that keepeth his commandments dwelleth in Him and He in Him.

6. As we combine the Love and Faith message we are trusting God's love for our needs and his love automatically flows through us to others.

7. Instead of a "name it and claim it message as some of the Body of Christ understood it, <u>Love and Faith is a "Crucifixion" message, a dying to what we want so that God can do what He wants</u>. Only then can the love and power of God be manifested to others through us, bringing us the abundant (more than is needed) life.

8. Love and faith when used together will restore us to the joy of our youth. It will make us fly like eagles. We will experience in reality some of the glories of heaven on earth for one reason only ... GOD LOVES US SO MUCH, HE WANTS TO BLESS US!

Confusion On The Path

CHAPTER 11

My sister and brother, please listen to me ... especially if you are one of God's children who love Him with all of your heart and desire to be in perfect obedience to Him. If this is your greatest desire, the devil will use that desire as a weapon against you.

As a baby Christian filled with the Holy Spirit, God will lead and guide you in many different ways. He will speak so clear to you and give you signs that are so meaningful to you, that you always know exactly the direction He wants you to go and what He wants you to do. During this time, He may speak to you about events that will happen in the future in your life. This blessed event may cause you some problems if you do not understand a few guidelines of importance that are necessary when you communicate with God.

Due to the lingering manifestations of the old sin nature in our mind, emotions and will, we may not always be in tune perfectly with God. Therefore, we may not always hear God as clear or as correct as we should. God's timing is usually different than what we think we heard. Abraham heard God, but he had no idea he would have to wait until he was 100 years old to have a son. We tend to get discouraged if God's timetable is different than ours.

When God shares a future event with you, do not go around telling everyone what God said unless He tells you specifically to do so. Many times we do not hear Him exactly right. If the event does not occur as we said it would, everyone thinks we are crazy. Our non-Christian friends are pushed away from God. We think God let us down. If God said it will happen, it will happen. In due season, you will hear Him clearly.

If we depend upon God constantly to tell us or give us signs to direct our actions, we are in big trouble. God can and will do this from time to time. However, as He begins to move us from the baby stage to maturity, He moves us from a guidance walk into a faith walk with Him. This means gradually, for a season, He will no longer guide us with His words or with outward signs. Instead, He begins to teach us to trust His love and to step out in faith to do the next right thing, believing He has already gone before us.

The trouble occurs when a child of God is so afraid of not doing God's will that without realizing it, he is not willing to enter the faith walk. He still wants signs to show him direction so he will do God's will. He loves God so much he does not want to hurt Him. Yet, he is hurting Him, because without faith you cannot please God.

When God stops giving signs and the child of God stops moving, he or she is stuck on the top of the fence that separates God's way from man's way. This person has one foot on each side. He is not enough into the world to be successful and he is not enough into God's way to be blessed. He feels there is a wall in front of him. He does not know in which direction to go or what to do. He remembers God's promises to him that seem so impossible. He is holding on to these promises. His faith is in them and herein lies the problem.

When God stops giving signs and the Christian stops and will not move without signs, a vacuum is created and the demons of hell run right into it. They come as angels of light and start giving all types of signs. As the Christian starts accepting the false signs as God's signs, he is carried along a path that leads to total bondage. I walked that path for nine years. It is hell! As I look back on it, I was like a rabbit that kept finding a carrot every so often in front of me. I kept looking for the next carrot, and the next, and the next until I was led into total bondage. I did not know how to get out. I had followed signs for so long that without a sign, I could not move. I remembered all of the promises of God, but few of them became a reality in my life. My family and friends thought I was crazy ... and I was. I had been deceived by the devil because I wanted to do God's will so bad. I would not move unless I got a sign or God told me exactly what to do.

How do you get out of this mess or how do you help someone else who is caught in this trap to get out? It is hard to do! First of all, the person is blinded and cannot see that he is caught in a trap. He will tell you all of the miraculous signs and wonders God has given him. Second, how can we really be sure that the person is being deceived? I am sure everyone thought Noah was crazy when he started building a large boat miles and miles from the nearest ocean. But, he had heard God clearly!

Here is the best way to identify the problem. Look at the person's life. Does he have peace or is he constantly getting upset with God because God is not doing what He promised He would do. Does he really know God's word, believe it and confess it? Is he always talking about "what God told him" or the latest sign God gave him or is he sharing the good news and love of God with others? If you feel you may be in bondage, **START PRAISING GOD FOR IT.** Why? Because the very problem a child of God is permitted to walk through is the exact area of ministry that God will use the person in, to "feed His lambs and feed His sheep."

Begin a simple program of fasting from some of the pleasures of this world. Ask the Holy Spirit to draw you to prayer and Bible study and step out to do it. Pick up all of the promises and signs you feel God has given you and lay them at His feet. Use S.T.P. on them! Let go of them! God does not want you to have faith in them. He wants you to have faith in His word which will lead you to His love. Do not feel that if they are of God, by letting go of them, they will never happen. Actually, if they are of God, the very reverse will occur. You have been holding on to them so tight that they have become your first love. They are standing between you and God. This is why you find it so hard to hear God anymore. God works in this way. We must be willing to give up all to get all. We must die to self to live. After you have put everything at His feet ... now trust His love. Each day get up and do the next right thing. A Christian's life should be a continuous line of little "next right things" connected by praise and thanksgiving. Even the biggest problem or tragedy is just another "small next right thing" if we are in constant communion with our Lord.

As we step out to do the next right thing, with no thought for the past or future or even for the promises we think God spoke to us, God will change our mourning into dancing. He will restore the joy of our youth. He will restore all that the cankerworms have eaten up.[34] We will be a blessing to ourselves and to others and the joy of the Lord will be our strength. We will never be alone! I have found that those things I thought I could never live without, pale in comparison to the wondrous blessings our Lord Jesus uses to fulfill the desires of my heart.

God's Message To You

CHAPTER 12

My child, please listen to Me. I want you to rest in My love. The way you rest in My love is to let go of what you want and let Me do what I want to do in your life. This means you must be <u>willing</u> to walk away from what you are doing or possess that is not of me and not only never look back, but not even care one bit that you have left the object of your affection.

My child, to do this takes a special grace from Me. It is the same grace that sets a person free from any addiction. I give My children that grace when I see that their heart is turned toward Me instead of the addiction, problem or need.

When they have set their will to be free and <u>desire</u> to be free with all of their heart, then <u>as they trust My love to keep them free, I free them.</u>

They will stay free as long as their will is toward Me and away from the addiction. If they gradually begin to permit their mind to think on the pleasure of the addiction or the worries of a problem, without them realizing it, <u>their will begins to change very gradually.</u> Slowly, it turns away from Me to an increasing longing for the pleasures of the addiction or the worry and concern over the problem.

As their will changes from a desire for Me to a feeling of sorrow because they can no longer enjoy the pleasure of the addiction or they no longer trust My love to meet their need, at that moment, I have to let go of them and immediately they will fall back into total bondage.

The same thing is true of you in every area of your life. If you desire to draw closer to Me, to rest in My love, to really desire and will to do it, I will set you free from every concern you have in every area of your life. S.T.P. is the **PATH!**

As long as your will is toward any specific object of affection or problem in your life, I cannot draw you closer to Me in that particular area. My blessings cannot flow to you in any area of your life in which I am not your first love.

My child, if you will turn your will toward Me in every area of your life that you feel stress or experience bondage, I will bless you. If you will set your will to turn from the things of this world that tend to draw you away from Me, I will set you free and give you a peace that passes all understanding.

I will restore you completely! I will bless you and bless you. I will answer your every prayer. I will open every door. I will set you free! I will flow through you like rivers of living water to people who know Me and do not know Me. I will bless everything you set your hand to.

My child, here is how you turn your will to Me on a specific subject. First, you must use your mind to direct your thoughts toward Me whether you feel like it or not. It must be done by an act of your will (a total surrender).

It is a deliberate turning away from what you want ... what you are trying to accomplish ... what is worrying you, causing you stress. It is a deliberate turning of your mind toward Me, <u>not to get Me to help you do what you want done,</u> but to permit Me to do what I want to do in the situation. I planned your life. I know exactly what it will take in your life to get you in a position where I can bless you.

You must stop thinking about the situation or problem. You must get your eyes on Me ... on My word. Only then will you know exactly what I have said I will do for you when you need help. I do not lie! I must have your trust in My Love!

When you turn your eyes and thoughts to Me the action will be very painful, at times. You will be deliberately walking away from the very thing, situation, or concern that means so much to you.

To totally give up a situation and walk away from it, to leave where your treasure has been so long, in order to see what I want to do in your life, to rest in My love, to listen to My thoughts and desires, to do My will, all of these things are how you return My love in a perfect way. I will meet <u>every</u> need in <u>every</u> area of your personal, home and business life. I do not lie! The works were <u>FINISHED</u> before the world was ever made.

My child, I am ready to separate you from the world! I am ready to separate My children from the world. It all starts with an act of your will to "desire" to return to your <u>FIRST LOVE</u> and to do the <u>FIRST WORKS</u> that you did when you gave your life to Me. You repented of your sins. Now you need to repent of "UNBELIEF" because over and over you have failed to trust Me and My love to supply your needs.

I need the same turning of your will over to Me. I need the same letting go, only this time it is not just your spiritual life I want, but every area of your being.

I desire to remove <u>"SELF"</u> from you in every way. To do that, I must have your will <u>in every area of your life.</u> I am not asking you to give up all and become inactive. In truth, when you are willing to give up all, you get all! Your activity will increase because I have much to do through you.

I will <u>always</u> send you people who can do the very things you desire to do, if those things have been put in your heart by Me.

STEPS TO LIBERTY

1. <u>Remove</u> your eyes from the situation, person, desire, feeling or thought and look at Me. You cannot make yourself **forget** the situation or how you feel about it, but by an act of your will, you can take your eyes off of the situation and look at Me ... at my love. **STOP LOOKING AT THE PROBLEM OR SITUATION, NO MATTER HOW CRITICAL IT IS. LOOK AT ME! SAY JESUS ... JESUS.**

2. As you look at Me, make a cold business decision to desire to give up, let go, walk away from, stop worrying about the addiction, problem or situation that is driving you to spend all of your thoughts or time on it.

3. Then begin to think about whether or not this addiction or concern that you have had toward the person, place or thing adds any real value for the life you will spend with Me for eternity.

   <u>You will find the only true thing that will have value for you for all eternity is the time you spend resting in My love.</u> Only then can I do

what My Father planned for Me to do in you and through you, which is to bless you and others in many different ways. The blessings will flow through you automatically.

4. As your thoughts reveal the uselessness of the addictive situation as it relates to value in eternity, your desire for it will vanish. At this point, make a cold business decision to turn away from the addiction, let go of it completely. Instead, place your DESIRE AND LOVE on Me instead of the addiction.

5. At this point, make a verbal confession to Me that you are willing to give up the addiction or situation completely and hand it to Me just as you did your life. Then, I shall take it and <u>in due season</u>, set you free from it.

6. Now, <u>trust My Love.</u> Look at My word. <u>Praise Me and thank Me</u> that I always meet your need abundantly through My Son, Jesus Christ. I am your Father and I love you.

My child, I want all of you, not part. I have part now. I need all of you before I can flow through you to others with all of My power and glory. <u>Start today and turn from the things that have no value for eternity.</u> **I will be with you!**

God's Roller Coaster Ride To Maturity

CHAPTER 13

A MATURING CHRISTIAN HAS BEEN PLACED ON A ROLLER COASTER RIDE TO MOLD US INTO THE IMAGE OF JESUS.

Our life is like a roller coaster … a big one. When you are on a roller coaster, as you go up the incline, you can rest, let loose of the bar or whatever you are holding on to and relax. This period represents the times in our life when we have no stress, no major problems or situations. We are at peace … resting in God's love.

Then, as the roller coaster car reaches the top and begins to careen wildly down its track, flipping us upside down, twisting us beyond what it seems we can stand, putting us on the very edge of thinking surely we shall perish, we hold onto the safety bar for dear life.

This ride down the coaster represents the period in our life when circumstances are overwhelming us, when our failures are beyond belief, when sin makes us think we are choosing the world, the flesh and the devil instead of Jesus, when so many decisions and problems confront us that we truly feel we are perishing.

Just as we hold onto the safety bar on our ride down the roller coaster incline, we hold onto the love of God for dear life. We literally **"Cling to His Love!"** We trust His love that no matter what is happening to us, it is working for our good according to His purpose. This is what Psalm 91:14-16 is all about ... **"Clinging to His Love"** and **"Acknowledging His Authority"** ... believing in due season He will turn every one of our lemons into lemonade.

THIS IS WHY HE GAVE US S.T.P.

SO WE CAN "LIVE PERFECT IN JESUS" FOREVER.

GOD'S SPECIAL PROMISE TO YOU

PSALM 91:14-16 Our Lord says to **You!** *"Because you have placed yourself <u>to cling to My love,</u> therefore I will deliver you. I will set you on high because you have <u>acknowledged My authority.</u>*

"You shall call upon Me and I will answer you. I will be with you in trouble. I will deliver you and make you great.

"With long life I will satisfy you and show you My salvation."(Salvation in the Hebrew is deliverance, health, victory and prosperity)

WE CLING TO GOD'S LOVE AND ACKNOWLEDGE GOD'S AUTHORITY WHEN WE USE S.T.P. AND DIE TO WHAT WE WANT!

NOTE: If this message has kindled a desire in your heart to learn more about the power of praise, I strongly suggest you purchase a book entitled, *Prison to Praise* by Merlin Carothers, 1970, Merlin R. Carothers, Escondido, CA., at any Christian book store. It was on the national best sellers list for 210 weeks and millions have been printed. The book demonstrates over and over by miracles upon miracles that God is faithful to those who Surrender, Trust and Praise. Although Rev. Carothers talks only of praise, in every miraculous situation, you will see surrender and trust were a part of the miracle.

ONE LAST THOUGHT FOR US TO CONSIDER AS WE WALK THE PATH

Hebrews 10:25 says that we should not forsake the assembling of ourselves together for the purpose of exhorting, encouraging and helping each other.

Many times we say we go to church to worship God with prayers, songs, and the preaching of the Word. Based on the scripture above, in reality, the gathering together is not *worship* but *fellowship*.

The only *true* worship we can give God is when we trust His love for ALL of our needs and reach out to be a blessing to others.

In Matthew 15:8, Jesus said that many draw near Him with their mouths and honor Him with their lips, but their hearts are far from Him. How many times do we praise God in church and then fail to trust His love for our needs the rest of the week?

In John 4:20-24, Jesus told the woman at the well that the time would come when true believers would not worship the Father in a specific location, but rather they would worship in Spirit and in Truth.

"Spirit and Truth" is not a building, but a condition and attitude of the heart which brings forth Surrender, Trust, and Praise in the midst of a trial or need, based solely upon knowledge of God's love.

Fellowship with believers is a must for us! Worship is a must for God! Maturity in the Christian life is a combination of both.

Have you...have I....somehow mistaken fellowship for worship? Have we failed to enter the position of S.T.P. so that God's abundant life can flow in us and through us to others?

SHARE YOUR TESTIMONY

As you use S.T.P., God will make himself known to you in a very real way. Please share God's miraculous works with us and others. Let us know if we can share your experiences on our website. Also let us know if we can use your name or if you prefer to remain anonymous. Thank You.

Contact Us at:

email: Don@afellowtravelor.com

Website: www.afellowtravelor.com

or

send your letter to:

Don Hunt

4020 Jordonia Station Road

Nashville, TN 37218

Jesus Christ Loves You and Will Never Give Up On You

No matter what you do to yourself, to your loved ones, to your enemies, Jesus Christ loves you and will never give up on you.

His love is always reaching out to you. All you must do to receive this Love is to accept His Love. Say this now, say it out loud if possible. "Thank you Jesus. I accept your Love. I accept your will for my life."

Jesus Christ died for your sins and thereby gave you eternal life. Now tell our Lord you accept His free gift of eternal life and surrender your will to His will.

All through the day repeat over and over "Thank you Jesus," and Jesus will give you inner peace that will surpass your most cherished earthly dreams.

Jesus Christ is alive today and the Bible is "The Word". Admit your needs, accept Him into your life and change your world. Read the word of God daily and learn the truth.

Jim Hunt,
Chairman
Buffet Pizza Company, LLC
jhunt@buffetpizza.com

Scripture References

1. JOHN 10:10 ... *"I am come that they might have life and that they might have it more abundantly."*

2. REVELATION 3:20 ... *"Behold, I stand at the door, and Knock. If any man (or woman) hear my voice and open the door, I will come into him, and will sip with Him and He with me."*

3. EPHESIANS 2:8-9 ... *"For by grace are ye saved through faith and that not of yourselves. It is the gift of God. Not of works, lest any man should boast."*

4. JOHN 10:27-28 ... *"My sheep hear my voice, and I know them and they follow me And I give into them eternal life, and they shall never perish, neither shall any man pluck them out of my hand."*

5. ROMANS 5:1 ... *"Therefore, being justified by faith, we have peace with God, through our Lord Jesus Christ."*

6. HEBREWS 3:12 ... *"Take heed brethren, lest there be in any of you an evil heart of unbelief, in departing from the living God."*

7. PHILIPPIANS 4:19 ... *"but my God shall supply all your need according to His riches in glory by Christ Jesus."*

8. 2 Chronicles 20:1-22 … (Please read verses 1-21) verse 22: *"And when they began to sing and praise, the Lord sat ambushments against the children of Am'mon, Mo'eb and mount Se'ir, which were come against Judah and they were smitten."*

   Acts 16:25-34 Paul and Silas prayed and sang praises into God . An earthquake shook the foundations of the prison and the doors were opened . Their bands were loosed and the keeper of the prison and all of His family came to believe in Jesus and His power.

9. EPHESIANS 2:10 … *"For we are His workmanship, created in Christ Jesus,unto good works, which God hath before ordained, that we should walk in them."*

10. ROMANS 8:28 … *"And we know that all things work together for good to them that love God, to them who are the called, according to His purpose."*

11. 1 TIMOTHY 1:5 … *"Now the end of the commandment (faith) is charity (Love), out of a pure heart, and of a good conscious, and of faith unfeigned."*

12. HEBREWS 4:3 … *"For we which have believed do enter into rest, as He said, as I have sworn in my wrath, if they shall enter into my rest, although the works were finished from the foundation of the world."*

13. JAMES 1:2-4 … *"My brethren, count it all joy when you fall into divers temptations, knowing this, that the trying of your faith worketh patience. But let patience have her perfect work, that ye may be perfect and entire, wanting nothing.*

14. PHILIPPIANS 2:13-14 ... *"For it is God which worketh in you both to will and to do of His good pleasure. Do all things without mourning and disputing."*

    EPHESIANS 5:20 ... *"Giving thanks always for all things into God and the Father in the name of our Lord Jesus Christ."*

15. PSALM 30:11 ... *"Thou hast turned for me my mourning into dancing. Thou hast put off my sackcloth and girded me with gladness."*

16. PSALM 50:23 ... *"Whose offereth praise glorified me and to him that ordereth his conversation aright will I show the salvation of the Lord."*

17. ROMANS 12:3 ... *"for I say, through the grace given into me, to every man that is among you, not to think of himself more highly than he ought to think. But to think soberly, according as God hath dealt to every man the measure of faith."*

18. 2 PETER 1:4 ... *"Whereby are given into us exceedingly great and precious promises, that by these ye might be partakers of the divine nature."*

19. TITUS 3:5 ... *"Not by works of righteousness which we have done, but according to His mercy, He saved us by the washing of regeneration (Salvation) and renewing(restoration) of the Holy ghost."*

20. HEBREWS 13:15 ... *"By Him (Jesus),therefore let us offer the sacrifice of Praise to God continually, that is the fruit of our lips, giving thanks to His name."*

    PSALM 107:21-22 ... *"Oh that men would praise the Lord for his goodness, and for His wonderful works to the children of men. And let them sacrifice the sacrifice of thanksgiving and declare His works with rejoicing."*

21. EXODUS 17:11 ... *"and it came to Pass, when Moses held up His hand that Israel prevailed and when he let down his hand, Amalek (the enemy) prevailed."*

22. MARK 11:23-24... (Jesus speaking).... *"For verily I say into you, that whosoever shall say into this mountain (problem), be thou removed and be thou cast into the sea, and shall not doubt in His heart, but shall believe that those things which he saith shall come to pass, he shall have whatsoever he saith. Therefore I say into you, what things soever ye desire when you pray, believe that ye receive them and ye shall have them."*

23. HEBREWS 10:14 ... *"For by one offering (death and resurrection), He (Christ) hath perfected forever then that are sanctified* (made Holy)."*

24. EPHESIANS 4:13 ... *"Till we all come in the unity of the faith, and of the knowledge of the Son of God, unto a perfect man, unto the measure of the stature (greatness) of the fullness of Christ."*

25. HEBREWS 11:6 ... *"But without faith it is impossible to please Him (God), for he that cometh to God must believe that He is (God), and that He is a rewarder of them that diligently seek Him."*

26. MATTHEW 17:20 ... *"And Jesus said into them... because of your unbelief. For verify I say into you. If you have faith as a grain of mustard seed, ye shall say unto this mountain, remove hence to yonder place and it shall remove and nothing shall be impossible unto you."*

27. GALATIANS 2:16 ... *" Knowing that a man is not justified by the works of the law, but by the faith of Jesus Christ."*

28. HEBREWS 4:9-10 ... *"there remaineth therefore a rest to the people of God. For he that is entered into His rest, he also hath ceased from his own works, as God did from His."*

29. 2 CORINTHIIANS 5:17-18 ... *"Therefore if any man be in Christ, he is a new creature. Old things are passed away. Behold all things are made new."*

30. HEBREWS 10:35-36 ... *"Cast not away therefore your confidence, which hath great recompense of reward. For ye have need of patience, that after ye have done the will of God, ye might receive the promise."*

31. ROMANS 1:16-17 ... *"For I am not ashamed of the Gospel of Christ. For it is the power of God unto Salvation to everyone that believeth. To the Jew first and also to the Greek. For therein is the righteousness Of God revealed (in us) from faith to faith as it is written. The just shall live by faith."*

    Salvation: Strong's concordance... G 4991... rescue or safety. (physically or morally), deliver, health.

    1 PETER 2:24 ... *"Who His own self (Jesus), bore our sins in His own body on the tree, that we being dead to sins, should live unto righteousness, by whose stripes ye were healed."*

    Healed: Strong's Concordance ... G-2390 ... to cure, heal, make whole.

32. MATTHEW 22:36-40 ... *"'Master, which is the great commandment in the Law?' Jesus said into him. 'Thou shalt love the Love thy God with all thy heart, and with all thy soul, and with all thy mind. This is the first and great commandment. And the second is like into it. Thou shalt love thy*

neighbor as thyself. <u>On these two commandments hang all the law and the prophets.</u>'"

33. <u>PSALM 5:11-12</u> ... *"But let all those that put their trust in thee rejoice. Let them ever shout for joy, because thou defendest them. Let them also that love thy name be joyful in thee. For thou Lord, wilt bless the righteousness. With favor wilt thou compass him as with a shield."*

34. <u>JOEL 2:25</u> ... *"And I will restore to you the years that the locust hath eaten, the cankerworm, and the caterpillar, and the palmerworm, my great army, which I sent among you."*

35. <u>GALATIANS 2:20</u> ... *"I am crucified with Christ, nevertheless I live yet not I, but Christ liveth in me. And the life, which I now live in my body (flesh), <u>I live by the faith of the Son of God,</u> who loved me and gave himself for me."*

36. ROMANS 8:14-17 ... *"For as many as are led by the Spirit of God, they are the sons of God"* (Have the nature of God). *"For ye have not yet received the spirit of bondage again to fear, but ye have received the spirit of adoption, whereby we cry Abba Father. The spirit itself beareth witness with our spirit, that we are the children of God; and if children, then heirs, heirs of God, and joint heirs with Christ; if so be that we suffer with him, that we may be also glorified together."*